Little Bird
Learns To FLY

Written By **Marni Allison**
Illustrated By **Lorraine Shulba**

Little Bird Learns to Fly
Copyright @ 2020 Marni Allison
Transformthejourney.com
marni@transformthejourney.com

Graphic Design, Cover Design & Illustrations by Lorraine Shulba – www.bluebugstudios.com

All rights reserved. Printed in the United States of America and Canada. No part of this book may be used or reproduced in any manner whatsoever without written permission from the author, except in the case of brief quotations within critical articles or reviews.

Although the author and publisher have made every effort to ensure that the information in this book was correct at press time, the author and publisher do not assume and hereby disclaim any liability to any party. Further, we assume no responsibility for errors or omissions in the information in this book. The ideas expressed here are based on the author's own experiences, opinions and imagination. The author and publisher are neither doctors nor in the position of registered authorities to give you expert advice. Use this information as you see fit at your own risk.

Published by Get You Visible
http://www.getyouvisible.com/
Print ISBN: 978-1-989848-18-0

DEDICATION

This book is dedicated to the "greats" in my life: Nahanni, River, Kaizen, Tanek, Orion, Jettlyn, Nova, Marlowe, Etta, Audrey, Maryn, and the little one on his way, who remind me why it is so important to share the best version of myself with others.

ACKNOWLEDGEMENTS

Little Bird wrote itself, but an editor made it brilliant. Allissa Blondin's diligence made Little Bird's words sing, and ensured the story had wings to make it meaningful. I discovered that writing prose is excruciatingly difficult, but Allissa's "bird grid" ruled the roost!

Lorraine Shulba captured the imagery and emotion of the story. She brought Little Bird to life, handled her with love and care, and a healthy dose of humor. See more of her award-winning art at www.bluebugstudios.com.

Little Bird would have stayed a poem perched in my travel journals, if not for the encouragement of Lisa McDonald, Joanne Yee, and Wendy Sells. A special thank you to Maureen Grabarczyk for the many sessions scouring a thesaurus and for contributing to the story and to my life.

"This MASTERPIECE of a book is not intended to be a hidden gem. Rather, *Little Bird Learns To Fly* should be enjoyed by all! Little Bird resides within all of us, easily comparable to that of our inner child. I am a staunch believer that it is our inherent responsibility as adults to remain bravely connected to our Little Bird Spirit, for it is within that wondrous and adventurous space that we are afforded the courage to take flight and spread our wings in this journey we call life. The profound lessons contained within this book will inevitably transform your soul, expand your mind, and deepen your heart, while transcending your highest level of personal ascension, on the trajectory for richer meaning and purpose. A resounding bullseye has been struck by author Marni Allison!"

Lisa McDonald, Living Fearlessly with Lisa McDonald

FOREWORD

Little Bird's journey began on an island in Indonesia, when I was awakened one morning by a bird singing outside my window. Loudly. Persistently. Urgently. Half asleep, a poem formed in my mind, in rhythm with the bird's insistent chirps. I grabbed my iPad and began typing, capturing what I imagined this songbird was saying.

When the bird finally stopped chirping, and the words stopped flowing, I'd written a short story in prose. It was a tale about a little bird, who was torn between following expectations, or casting off those limitations and exploring the world. As I was reading this little bird's adventures, I quickly realized it was an autobiography. I also noticed the answers to the questions that had been lingering in my mind for months were found within its pages. Questions such as: Is there something more I'm supposed to do or say… something more I'm supposed to learn… something more I'm supposed to contribute?

You might think *Little Bird Learns to Fly* is a story about travel. And you'd be partly right, but mostly wrong. When I shared the story with friends, they recognized my ventures within its pages, but they also expressed how Little Bird's journey mirrored their own lives. That's when the magic began.

Little Bird's story embodies a powerful, universal experience because it represents everyone's journey. The journey of casting aside our limiting beliefs, and choosing to live consistent with our own values. The journey of moving beyond our comfort zones, and embracing challenges, big and small. The journey of searching for our purpose, and exploring who we are at our core.

I want you to experience this book, not just read it. Speak the words out loud as you read them, and listen for the rhythm and the musicality of the phrases. Absorb and explore the colors and visual imagery of the artwork. Close your eyes and imagine yourself visiting the locations set out before you. Attune yourself to the relationships within the story, and feel the emotions that bubble up inside of you. Take note of the themes that apply to your own life. Choose to use Little Bird's lessons to empower and uplift you in your own journey. To help you get the most out of this book, I've included questions to stimulate reflection, following the story.

But please don't stop there! Next, share the story… twice.

First, read the story to a child. Explore the pictures on the page and invite them to share what they see, help them discover the lessons, let them ask you questions, and ask them questions in return. Help them understand the words that are beyond their vocabulary by sharing what that word or phrase means to you. An interactive reading experience will, in itself, be a unique and fun adventure.

Then share the story with a young person who is starting a new stage of life, or discovering their own independence, such as a graduate from high school or university, or an adventurer departing on a voyage of their own. This story is a gift that they will surely treasure, as they explore who they want to be and how they will get there. I've also included questions at the end of the story to spark meaningful discussions with both children and young adults.

Now, it's time for you to discover how Little Bird learned to fly...
Marni xox

*L*ittle Bird was a lively sort, with intelligent eyes, a quirky smile, and bright blue feathers.
She was surrounded by a loving family and friends from all around her community.
Adventurous and independent, she appreciated the needs and beliefs of others.
She worked at an interesting job and lived in a beautiful nest.
Although she often visited nearby forests, she was careful not to stray too far from home.
Little Bird was content, and she had everything a little bird could want.
Still, Little Bird **felt there was something more** she was supposed to do with her life.

When Little Bird flew over the pond in the city square on her way to work, she wondered, *What if I flew right instead of flying straight ahead? Where would I go and what would I do?*
On a flight around the neighborhood later that day, she asked her daddy the questions she had pondered.
"Oh no, Little Bird! You can't fly right," Daddy Bird explained.
"Why not?" asked Little Bird. "Because making a living is necessary if you want to buy all the things you love. Choose a job you like. Work hard, stay committed, and enjoy the fruits of your labor. That's how **success** comes true." Little Bird adored her daddy and accepted he was right. She excelled at her work and knew she was doing the right thing for her future. She flew straight ahead and did not turn right because ***her path was clear and defined.***

When Little Bird ate a delicious Sunday dinner at her parents' nest, she wondered,
What if I flew left instead of flying straight ahead? Who would love me?
Washing dishes after dinner, she asked her mommy what her thoughts were about such things.
"Oh no, Little Bird! You can't fly left," Mommy Bird protested.
"Why not?" asked Little Bird.
"Because being close to the birds you love is one of life's greatest treasures.
Visit us often. Spend the day at the beach with us and share holiday feasts together.
That's how **commitment** comes true."
Little Bird loved her mommy and knew she was right.
She spent time with her family and knew she was as important to them as they were to her.
She flew straight ahead and did not turn left because **her world was enveloped by love.**

When Little Bird swept her nest and stuffed it with fresh twigs, she wondered,
What if I flew up and down instead of flying straight ahead? What would I experience?
Gathering baskets of yummy worms with her brother one weekend, they chatted about her wonderings.
"Oh no, Little Bird! You can't fly up and down," Brother Bird warned.
"Why not?" asked Little Bird.
"Because to avoid danger you must know who is near and what is around you.
Enjoy the comfort of your life. Visit places you know and spend time with the birds you trust.
That's how **security** comes true."
Little Bird idolized her brother and believed he was right.
She followed the rules and knew that by staying safe she made others feel comfortable too.
She flew straight ahead and did not fly up and down because **home offered sanctuary.**

When Little Bird played a lively game of soccer with her friends, she wondered, *What if I twirled around and around instead of flying straight ahead? Who would I meet?*
After the match, her friends gathered round in chatter and Little Bird shared her thoughts.
"Oh no, Little Bird! You can't twirl around and around," Best Friend Bird advised.
"Why not?" asked Little Bird.
"Because happiness comes from getting to know the birds who share your interests. Appreciate the relationships in your life. Play games and share confidences with each other. That's how ***belonging*** comes true."
Little Bird valued her friend's advice and assumed she was right. She joined her friends to play whenever she could, and knew they cherished one another. She flew straight ahead and did not twirl around and around because ***friends filled her heart and home.***

When Little Bird took an environmental science class at the local university, she wondered, *What if I flew in the opposite direction instead of flying straight ahead? What would I learn?*
At the end of one class, she told her teacher about her thoughts on flying.
"Oh no, Little Bird! You can't fly in the opposite direction," Master-Teacher Bird persuaded.
"Why not?" asked Little Bird.
"Because education teaches you how the world works and explains all you need to know. Listen to and learn from experts. Read important journals and books and watch documentaries. That's how ***knowledge*** comes true."
Little Bird admired her teacher and was convinced he was right.
She studied birds, trees, flowers, and bees, and knew she could find any answers she needed.
She flew straight ahead and did not fly in the opposite direction because
learning brought the world to her doorstep.

When Little Bird attended church or watched television shows and movies, she wondered, *What if I flew in a zig zag instead of flying straight ahead? What would I believe?*
She posted the question to her online book club and asked her friends to comment.
"Oh no, Little Bird! You can't fly in a zig zag," Story-Teller Bird responded.
"Why not?" asked Little Bird.
"Because having convictions defines who you are and provides a path for you to follow in life. Surrender your trust to those who hold the truth. Seek guidance through deep-rooted beliefs and rituals. That's how **consciousness** comes true."
Little Bird valued Story-Teller Bird and believed she was right.
She read sacred writings and listened to the news, and knew her beliefs aligned with others.
She flew straight ahead and did not fly in a zig zag because **society's scripts provided clarity.**

When Little Bird flew by schools, hospitals, or homeless shelters, she wondered,
What if I flew in every way possible instead of straight ahead? What would I achieve?
The answer she sought was revealed during a conversation at a charity dinner.
"Oh no, Little Bird! You can't fly in every way possible," Benevolence Bird recommended.
"Why not?" asked Little Bird.
"Because being part of a community means working with others to achieve a common good. Share your skills with others. Care for the infirm, teach the young, and assist those in need. That's how **contribution** comes true."
Little Bird respected Benevolence Bird and felt he was right.
She became a volunteer, and knew she was making a difference in the lives of others.
She flew straight ahead and did not fly in every way possible because
serving others made her happy.

Give with your heart

*L*ittle Bird got older and more subdued, a little rounder, and her tail feathers were edged with grey.
Mommy Bird and Daddy Bird had flown away, and Little Bird could not be with them anymore.
Brother Bird was busy with his own nest and family, and Best-Friend Bird was often away.
Little Bird was **busy and committed,** but occasionally overwhelmed by the needs of others.
She worked hard and owned a big, beautiful nest. She had visited many nearby forests.
Little Bird was comfortable, and she had everything a little bird was expected to want.
Still, Little Bird **believed there was something more** she was supposed to do with her life.

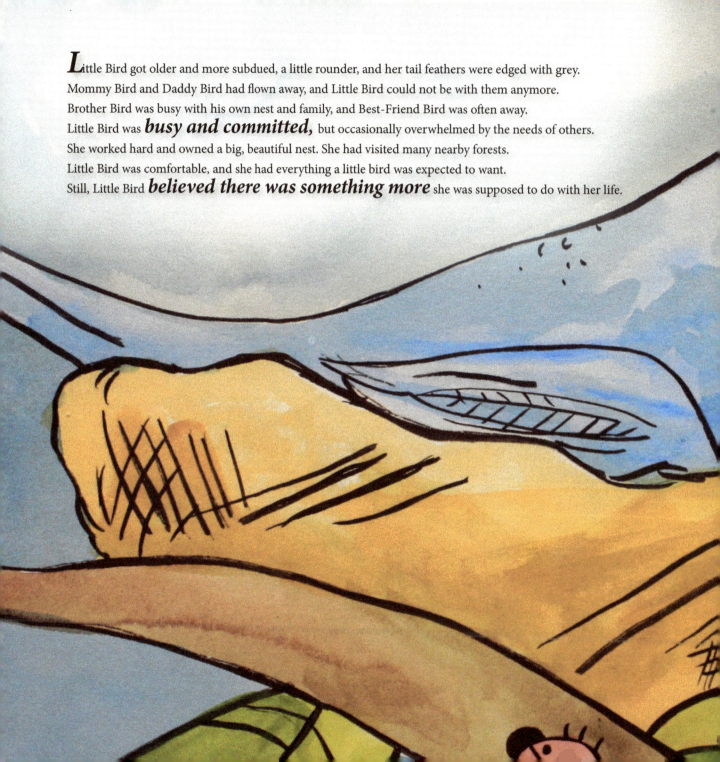

One day, when Little Bird flew by a tall, tall building all made of glass, she asked herself,
"*What if I fly straight ahead all of my life and don't turn in any way? How would I feel?*"
She looked at her reflection in the window to see if the desire for more showed on her face.
"Oh no, Little Bird! You can't always fly straight ahead," her reflection seemed to say.
"Why not?" asked Little Bird.
"Because change is only possible when you take action to do more with your life. Make a choice to fly differently. Learn to take risks and step outside of your comfort zone. That's how ***dreams*** comes true."
Little Bird acknowledged her desire for more and was optimistic she was right.
She packed her bags and knew if she was brave, she would experience something rewarding.
Instead of flying straight ahead, she turned right and
flew towards the unknown.

*F*lying right, Little Bird flew over far-away lands and visited nests of every shape and size.

But she wondered, *What if I fly right for too long? Will I forget how to fly home?*

She came upon an eagle wearing a weathered backpack and decided to ask her thoughts on the matter.

"Oh no, Little Bird! You won't forget how to fly home," World-Traveler Bird explained.

"Why not?" asked Little Bird.

"Because when you choose where to go and what to do, you develop purpose in your life.

Face new challenges head-on. Seek opportunities that test your skills, pride, and perseverance. That's how ***fulfillment*** comes true."

Little Bird was encouraged by World-Traveler Bird and was confident she was right.

She explored farms, cities and wetlands and knew she was discovering what really mattered to her.

She kept flying right because she knew **signposts would guide her when it was time to return home.**

Flying left, Little Bird fell in love with a kookaburra who loved to laugh.
But she wondered, *What if I fly too far left? Will I stop loving my family or will they stop loving me?*
That evening Little Bird shared her fears as she snuggled with her delightful companion.
"Oh no, Little Bird! You won't stop loving your family or they you," Beloved Bird soothed.
"Why not?" asked Little Bird.
"Because genuine love exists whether you are together or apart, and it endures even after death.
Commit to the birds you love. Accept their strengths and weaknesses, as they accept yours.
That's how **devotion** comes true."
Little Bird cherished Beloved Bird and acknowledged he was right.
She called home frequently and knew her family was happy to hear her excitement and joy.
She kept flying left because she knew **she was loved whether she was home or abroad.**

Flying up and down, Little Bird scaled the highest peaks and dived into bottomless seas.
But she wondered, *What if I fly up or fly down too sharply? Will I get hurt or fall into danger?*
As she put on a scuba mask, her dive master shed light on the matter, as only a kingfisher could.
"Oh no, Little Bird! You won't get hurt or fall into danger," Limitless Bird encouraged.
"Why not?" asked Little Bird.
"Because to achieve growth, you must act outside your comfort zone, but not beyond safety.
Act in spite of fear. Don't let fear of the unknown or the fears of others hold you back.
That's how **courage** comes true."
Little Bird was in awe of Limitless Bird and was convinced she was right.
She sang in a theatre and sat on a hippo's back, and she knew they were her choices to make.
She kept flying up and down because, **in spite of fear, she was flying higher than ever before.**

*T*wirling around and around, Little Bird camped with a colony of penguins for several weeks.
But she wondered, *What if I twirl around and around too fast? Will I lose my existing friends?*
Little Bird explained her trepidation at a beach party that weekend.
"Oh no, Little Bird! You won't lose your existing friends," Ambassador Bird assured.
"Why not?" asked Little Bird.
"Because true friends allow you to be yourself, authentic and imperfect, in good times and bad. They don't need you to conform to fit in. Honor your old friends and celebrate the new. That's how **connection** comes true."
Little Bird appreciated Ambassador Bird and agreed he was right.
She learned new songs and dances, and knew these were gifts of companionship and enrichment.
She kept twirling around and around because ***she was sharing the best version of herself with others.***

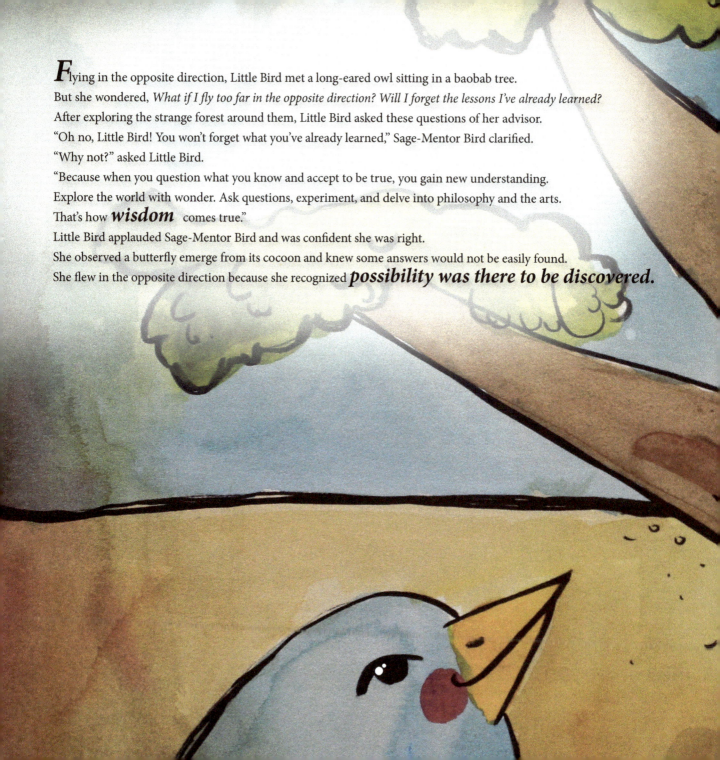

*F*lying in the opposite direction, Little Bird met a long-eared owl sitting in a baobab tree.
But she wondered, *What if I fly too far in the opposite direction? Will I forget the lessons I've already learned?*
After exploring the strange forest around them, Little Bird asked these questions of her advisor.
"Oh no, Little Bird! You won't forget what you've already learned," Sage-Mentor Bird clarified.
"Why not?" asked Little Bird.
"Because when you question what you know and accept to be true, you gain new understanding.
Explore the world with wonder. Ask questions, experiment, and delve into philosophy and the arts.
That's how **wisdom** comes true."
Little Bird applauded Sage-Mentor Bird and was confident she was right.
She observed a butterfly emerge from its cocoon and knew some answers would not be easily found.
She flew in the opposite direction because she recognized **possibility was there to be discovered.**

Flying in a zig zag, Little Bird listened to stories shared by an ostrich roaming the savanna.
But she wondered, *What if I fly in a zig zag too erratically? Will I lose the values that guide me?*
Sitting around the campfire listening to the ostrich elders, Little Bird shared her musings.
"Oh no, Little Bird! You won't lose your values," All-Perspectives Bird suggested.
"Why not?" asked Little Bird.
"Because universal truths reflect the values and principles that bind all birds together.
Accept love, offer hope, and seek guidance. Allow others to hold their own convictions.
That's how **enlightenment** comes true."
Little Bird was intrigued by All-Perspectives Bird and perceived he was right.
She respected other viewpoints and knew beliefs could change, but values would hold true.
She flew in a zig zag because ***the expectations of others no longer defined her.***

*F*lying in every way possible, Little Bird met a condor sunning herself on a mountaintop.
But she wondered, *What if I continue to fly in any way I choose? Will I become selfish and self-centered?*
The condor, who aspired to become a world traveler, contemplated Little Bird's questions.
"Oh no, Little Bird! You won't become selfish and self-centered," Next-Generation Bird stated.
"Why not?" asked Little Bird.
"Because when you empower yourself, others learn to recognize their own dignity and strength. Encourage others to fly. Light the path and help remove the barriers that keep them grounded. That's how ***legacy*** comes true."
Little Bird was inspired by Next-Generation Bird and welcomed her insight.
She beheld the panorama before her and knew having a purpose was about more than serving oneself.
She flew in every way possible because **it was within her power to champion others on their own journeys.**

Returning home, Little Bird flew by the tall, tall building all made of glass.
She asked herself, *"What if I stop flying in new and exciting ways?*
Have I found that something more I was longing for?"
She looked at her reflection in the window to see if the changes in her heart showed on her face.
"Oh no, Little Bird! You can't stop flying in new and exciting ways," her reflection seemed to say.
"Why not?" asked Little Bird.
"Because life evolves, with growth, loss, adventures and challenges, whether you seek change or not.
Be present in the moment. Acknowledge your choices and let go of anything that does not serve you.
That's how ***destiny*** comes true."
Little Bird reflected on her journey and knew she was right.
She flew beyond her comfort zone often and knew each time she did it had a ripple effect within.
She flew in new and exciting ways because **the prospect of transformation was the best part of flying.**

*L*ittle Bird felt so alive, with curious eyes, a quick smile, and blue tail feathers edged with grey.
She relished spending time with a growing flock of family and friends from all flights of life.
Although she felt affinity for the needs and beliefs of others, she stayed true to herself.
She ***found meaning*** at work and at home by contributing to purposes that would benefit others.
She appreciated her own forest but was never afraid to stray too far from home.
Little Bird was grateful, because she had everything a little bird would ever need.
Little Bird had discovered the most important lesson of flying:
every beginning leads to something more.

POSTWORD

My goal in writing *Little Bird Learns to Fly* is to inspire you to find that something more you've been searching for. I hope the questions that follow encourage you to let your curiosity take you to places you've never been, awaken the parts of you that have been waiting to come alive, and motivate you to take action toward finding whatever you have been looking for.

1) What challenges and opportunities have taught you to fly? Have you ever chosen a course of action because it was aligned with your family's or society's expectations?

2) Would you like to experience, learn or achieve something more in your life? If so, what would that look like for you?

3) What's holding you back from pursuing something more? Are you living life with courage, curiosity, and authenticity or staying in your comfort zone out of fear?

4) How would you feel if you achieved your dream of something more? How would you feel if you never took the chance?

5) With your something more in mind, what steps are necessary to get you started? It is never too late to do, learn, or become something more.

Visit www.transformthejourney.com for a deeper conversation about the themes presented in this book. You can join my online book club or get discussion ideas for your own club. You can read stories of others who have learned to fly, or you can choose to share your own experiences or aspirations. If you are looking to transform your own journey, I invite you to explore my START program.

GUIDING FUTURE GENERATIONS

Once you have shared the story with a child, and with a young person starting on an independent journey, know that your efforts will make an impact in their lives. If you haven't had a chance to share this story yet, I encourage you to take up the gauntlet.

Children may not have absorbed all the conditioning they will encounter in life, but you might be surprised at how early they start incorporating limitations. What messages are you sending to the children in your life? Sharing the story with children will help develop their skills to become better readers, it will encourage them to use their imaginations, and it is a fun way to show them all the possibilities life has to offer so they can reach for their something more. Use the questions below to translate the core messages into clear and simple principles and actions for children.

1) If you could fly any way you wanted, what would be your favorite way to fly?
2) If you could try something new, or be anything you wanted, what would it be?
3) What does Little Bird see and do when she flies in all the different ways?
4) What does Little Bird learn from each bird she meets?
5) Which birds would you like to meet? Why do you want to meet them?

Young people starting a new stage of life are often optimistic and idealistic, but they may struggle with the difference between making conscious choices, or merely following expectations. Help them discover that searching for something more is natural and healthy, not a sign of discontent, or lack of gratitude. Use the questions below to spark a discussion.

1) What do you love doing? What are you really good at? What do you dream of doing, learning, and achieving in your life?
2) What choices are you making and actions are you taking that are leading you to your dreams? Which ones currently align you with something different?
3) Do you feel you have a choice in following your dreams, or do you feel you must curtail some dreams to meet expectations set by yourself, your family and friends, or society?
4) Your dreams and desires may change at different points in your life. When is living in your "comfort zone" appropriate, and when is it worthwhile to muster up the courage to take risks?
5) How can the people who love you help you learn to fly in every way possible? What do you need to do to live a courageous and authentic life, while being sensitive to the hopes, dreams, and fears of the loved ones who guide you?

Through these questions, you are providing an opportunity for the child and young person to explore who they want to be, and determine the actions required to get them there. Just imagine the confidence, curiosity, and sense of purpose that might be imparted, if Little Bird's lessons are learned early in life. I encourage you to visit my website to share the discoveries you made during your discussions. You never know who you might help!

My wish for you, and the people you share this book with, is that it inspires all of you to learn to fly in every way possible. And I hope you start today. After all, as Little Bird discovered, every beginning leads to something more.

CPSIA information can be obtained
at www.ICGtesting.com
Printed in the USA
LVHW071805090221
678844LV00036B/1216